Mind Mapping

How to Create Mind Maps Step-By-Step

John S. Rhodes

Mind Mapping

How to Create Mind Maps Step-By-Step

Table of Contents

Introduction   7

Chapter 1: What is a Mind Map?   11

Chapter 2: Which Mind Map to Use   19

Chapter 3: Seven Magical Steps to Mind Mapping 29

Chapter 4: Speed Mind Mapping   37

Chapter 5: Mind Map Templates   43

Chapter 6: Moving Around Your Mind Map   55

Chapter 7: Mind Map Tactics 101   61

Chapter 8: Advanced Tactics   67

Chapter 9: Conclusion   87

Introduction

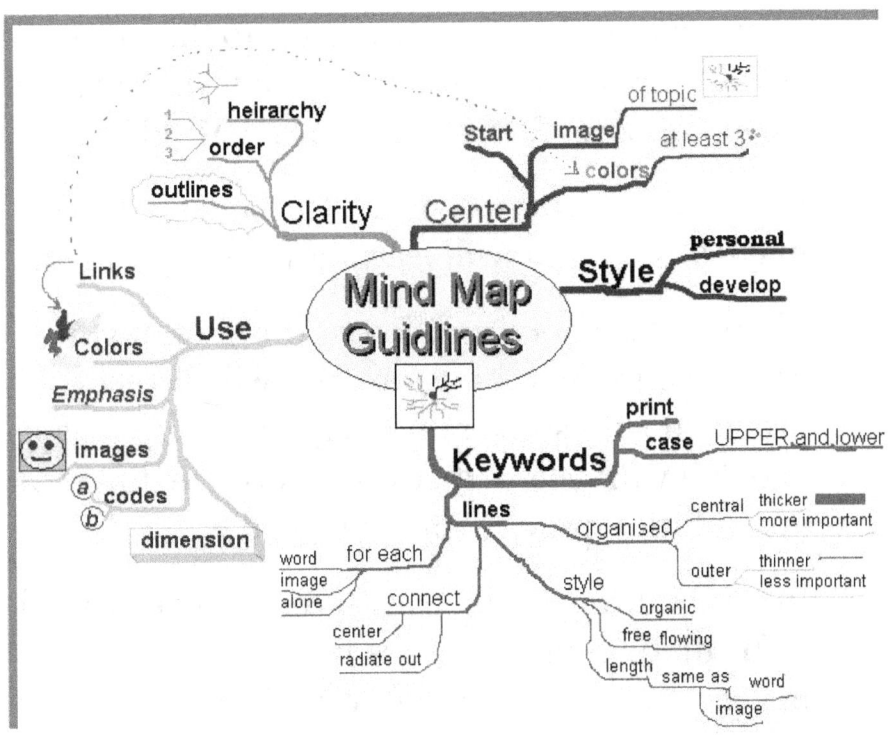

Welcome! This book is about mind mapping and, more specifically, **how to create mind maps**. There are nine different lessons within this book.

Chapter 1 asks, 'What is a Mind Map?' Within this chapter you are going to learn the difference between mind maps and mind mapping, as well as the correct way to create a mind map.

In Chapter 2, you are going to learn about the different software options as well as the different mind maps that can be utilized.

Chapter 3 is where you will get into the meat of actually creating a mind map. You will learn the 'Seven Magical Steps to Creating a Mind Map'.

In Chapter 4, you will be led through the seven magical steps and will learn how to apply them.

Chapter 5 covers the different things that you can use mind mapping for. You will also be provided with some mind mapping templates, and you will receive an overview of the different possibilities mind mapping provides.

In Chapter 6 you will learn how to move around your mind maps, as well as how to go back to make changes and edit after you have completed the first drafts.

Chapter 7 will demonstrate some of the tactics that you can use in mind mapping. In this chapter you will also learn some ways that you can apply mind mapping to your own life.

Chapter 8 is where you will get into some of the advanced techniques, along with being taught how to use mobile devices for mind mapping.

Finally, Chapter 9 will tie everything together for you.

Chapter 1: What is a Mind Map?

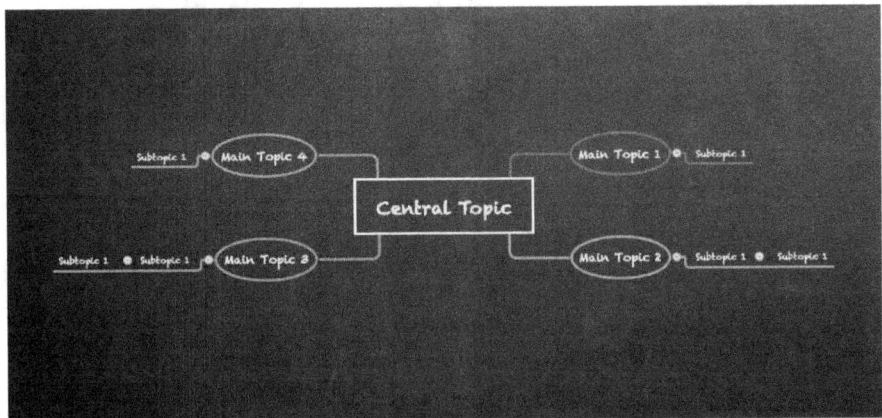

An example of a mind map is shown above. The box in the middle represents the 'Central Topic'. This is what you will begin with. Branching from the central topic are the main topics. Here they are represented with circles, but you could use any form or shape to represent your main topics. In the picture above there are four main topics, but you can have as many main topics as you like or need. You can think of these as ways to define your central topic. Arrows and lines are used to show the relationship between the central topics and the main topics.

A subtopic is branched out from each of the main topics in the example. More than one subtopic may branch out from each main topic in your own mind map. In Chapter 5 you will learn just how far this can go. In fact, it can go on forever! That is part of the beauty of a mind maps design; it is limitless.

Mind maps really can become quite large because a lot of times single words, or keywords, are used to represent larger ideas. Also, when only one topic is being described at a time, it takes a lot more boxes to describe and break apart a more complex idea or structure. Therefore, the more complex a mind map is, the larger it needs to be. This becomes particularly true when using mind mapping to brain storm.

Mind maps and mind mapping are not quite the same thing. A mind map is the document which is created as a result of the action of mind mapping. Mind maps can be created as .mm files. They can also be created in Word documents, as PDFs, or just sketched onto a normal piece of paper. This is another aspect of mind mapping that is really just endless. There are thousands, if not millions, of ways to create a mind map.

If mind maps are the result, then mind mapping is the activity. Mind mapping is what you use to organize your thoughts, the facts, multiple steps, or an entire process, so that you can collaborate with others or break apart a problem on your own. Think of mind mapping as the verb which creates the noun: the mind map.

One of the greatest things about mind maps is that the information is broken down into such a simple form that it helps you to remember. It also gives you a bird's-eye view of a problem, which allows you to see and understand that problem more easily. Furthermore, it can help you to break things up into easy-to-understand steps, which can make even complex tasks seem simple.

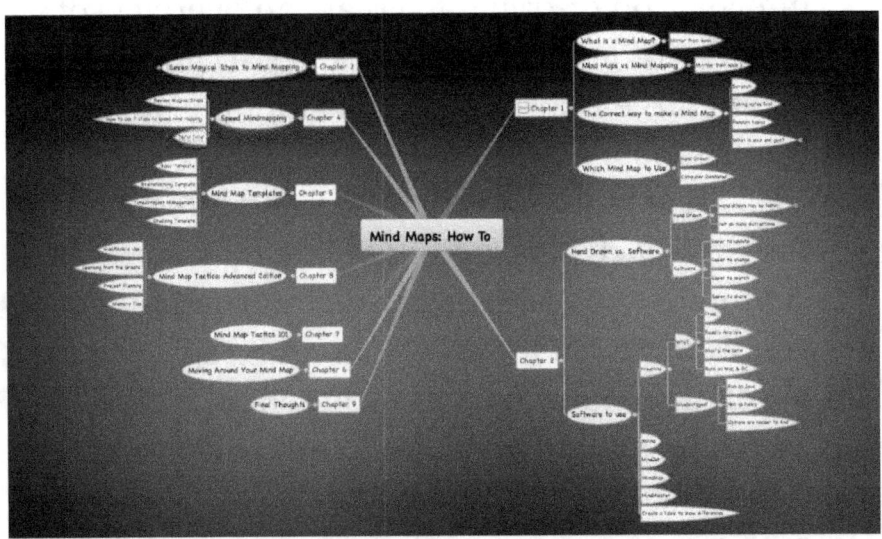

There are a few rules about mind mapping. For example, you are always supposed to have one central topic. The mind map above was used to outline this book. You can see that it contains a central topic and branching from the central topic are the various chapters. The 'proper' rules for creating a mind map will be covered in Chapters 3 and 4. However, the only "true" rule of mind mapping is that you should do it in the way that works best for you. When you're just starting out, you should probably follow the rules, but as you get more experience, feel free to deviate when it seems useful for you to do so.

There are three main ways that you can use a mind map:

You can use notes to create a mind map. This works best when you are organizing researched information or trying to create an overview of specific information. Say you were supposed to create three websites for a business. Your central topic may be something like 'Rhodes Inc.,' the main topics may be titled after each of the three websites, and then you may use the subtopics to organize specific information that you would want to include in each site. You may have taken notes on what your client wanted in each site, and organizing the information in a mind map would make it easier for you to set up each site or communicate to an assistant how it should be done.

The second method is to create your mind maps from scratch, using the creation as your note taking. This works well if you're taking notes in class or in a meeting. No matter what you are taking notes on, it's easy to write that topic in the middle and branch out with details from there. This also helps your mind to retain the information better. This way of organizing information, in most cases, works better than your typical top-to-bottom and left-to-right formats.

The final method for creating mind maps is a little bit more advanced. You create a mind map with the intent of linking seemingly random topics together. For instance, you can make a quick comparison of the similarities and differences between two rival websites. Your focus is on creating connections, rather than simply structuring information. This kind of mind mapping is a powerful tool for understanding complex systems.

Anytime that you sit down to create a mind map, the first question you should ask yourself is "What is my end goal?" Before you even begin, you want to have a good idea of what you want to achieve, what you want to learn, and for what purpose you want your mind map. However, if you are brainstorming, these goals may change as you move along, since mind maps have a way of making things more apparent and bringing out the bigger picture.

The ways that you can utilize mind maps are endless, as well. You can use them to communicate with others at work, for example, or you could use them to help you break down personal problems of your own. You can use it to make plans before selling your house, for breaking down the information in research papers before you begin writing, etc. No matter what you are doing, you need to have that end goal of what you want to achieve with your mind map before you begin. Otherwise, you could really get lost 'down the rabbit hole', so they say.

If you are reading this, then you should applaud yourself. Learning about mind mapping is a very smart thing to do. There is an infinite amount of ways that you can use mind maps to make your life better. The author's assumption is that you want to do just that. The rest of this book, therefore, is going to be geared to teaching you how to do that.

To a certain extent, we all have to structure information, whether we realize it or not. Since you have picked up this book, the author also assumes that you often have to structure information, and that you would like to learn a clearer, easier, and more efficient way to structure and organize that information. You may also want to be able to structure this information in a way that you can better communicate it with others. Learning to do so, in either or both cases, is going to make you more efficient.

On the other hand, you may just want to learn about mind mapping or add to what you already know. If this is true, that is great, too. Mind mapping and learning to use mind maps effectively can really help you to achieve far more than you could ever do without such a tool. So please, continue on to Chapter 2, where you can learn about some of the different mind mapping tools that you can utilize and get some insight into which types of mind maps are right for you.

Chapter 2: Which Mind Map to Use

Mind maps take two forms: hand-drawn and computer rendered. This chapter is going to compare the two and then describe some of the different options available for using each.

Hand-drawn mind maps were really what everyone used prior to the last couple of years, for the most part anyway. In other words, it was within the last couple of years that computer mind mapping really began to step into the forefront as one of the best ways to organize information.

Although computerized mind maps have opened up a great deal of options on how to create and use mind maps, hand-drawn mind mapping should by no means be disregarded. A hand-drawn mind map is very quick and easy to create. So, it definitely has its advantages. For example, if an idea hits you at Starbucks you could quickly jot it, and all the aspects of it, down on the back of a napkin in the time it takes for them to finish making your latte.

As stated above, hand-drawing your mind maps is going to be faster, especially when you are first starting out. Also, you are going to be able to zone into your hand-drawn work better and you won't have as many distractions. Typically, on a computer you have a whole lot of icons that need your attention, email notifications, and so on. When you are creating a mind map on a piece of paper, you can completely clear off your desk and just go to town writing, drawing, and brainstorming on your mind map.

Hand-drawn also has the advantage of simple ease of use. There is no interface to learn when hand-drawing a mind map, and you are limited only by your imagination (instead of by software).

Despite these numerous advantages, you will actually be better off creating mind maps using software. Computerized mind maps are much easier to update and change. They are also easier to search through, and easier to share. Computerized mind maps have incredible communication value. For instance, they are written out in text, so you don't have to worry about people being able to read your handwriting, and of course they are often much neater.

The software that you use is going to automatically allow you to compensate when you forget to add a title or when you need to add in another topic. Most of the time, if you forget something like this on a hand-drawn mind map, you end up having to redraw it in order to make it neat or to have enough room. Another great thing about this software is that it allows you to insert images. So, if you're the type that can't even draw a stick-figure very well, you're covered. This can be extremely effective, especially if you are trying to communicate your ideas to others.

The easy 'searchability' of computerized mind maps cannot be overstated. If you have a mind map that is huge, such as one that encompasses an entire business, this can be extremely helpful. Some of the largest companies in the world, such as Disney and Boeing Aircraft, have used mind maps to structure their business. These mind maps were enormous. For example, Boeing Aircraft's mind map was over 40 feet long, and it was on paper. Could you imagine having to find something on that mind map?

Mind maps help you find connections and associations, and software can assist with this practice... It allows you to not only search the document, but update the document and move things around as well. Again, if the information needs to be reorganized on a hand-drawn version, you would either have to erase everything or redraft all of it.

Computerized mind maps also make things easier because if you need to communicate your ideas, you can simply email the mind map to one of your colleagues. So, even if they are halfway across the country (or even the world), your ideas can be communicated swiftly and easily. Furthermore, they can then edit it, adding their own input, and shoot it right back to you.

So, using mind mapping software has a lot of advantages, especially if you plan to use mind maps professionally. However, when you are first starting out, it is best to just grab a piece of paper and begin creating a simple mind map. This will help you get the feel for it and get a better grasp on how it works. It is just much simpler to start out on paper. Eventually, you will want to start using software, though. Doing so is going to get you a lot further and it is going to make you a lot more productive.

	Price	Advantages	Disadvantages
Freemind	Free	Completely Free Offers most basic features	Interface isn't as nice Can be buggy
XMind	Free Basic Version	More features that Freemind Unlimited Maps	Limited export abilities (free version)
MindJet	$349	Online collaboration Business discount Best User Interface	Expensive
iMindMap	$99 - $249	Created by Tony Buzan iOS/Andriod Versions Online Syncing	Expensive
MindMeister	Free – Limited to three maps	No software to install Good feature set	Requires internet access Limited to 3 maps in free version

There are a lot of different mind mapping software options out there. The chart above compares just a few. The mind map that contains this chart was created using FreeMind. One of the advantages of this program is, well, it's free (hence the name). FreeMind is readily available, and it has nearly all of the options that most of the premium software of its kind is going to give you.

Another one of the advantages of FreeMind is it can be used by both Mac and PC users. So, if you're on a Mac and your colleague is on a PC, you are still going to be able to send the file back and forth.

FreeMind does have its disadvantages and limitations, however. For example, it runs on Java, and currently Java has a reputation for not being very secure. Even so, it's unlikely you will run into issues with FreeMind involving security.

Another one of the disadvantages of this program is that it is not as fancy as some other programs. Also, you are not going to have some of the same options that other premium programs will provide. Furthermore, in FreeMind, some options are harder to find.

You have to decide what options you actually want and need because some of the premium programs can be very expensive. FreeMind is a great program to use, and it is more than good enough for most people. Again, it is all a matter of what you prefer and what you need. So, let's take a look at some of the premium options. Some of the 'paid' options that you have include:

- XMind

- MindJet

- iMindMap

- MindMeister

XMind is kind of a compromise between FreeMind and some of the other paid options. XMind has a free option, but they don't allow you to export as a PDF. Not everyone is going to have the same mind mapping software as you, so this can create some problems. The paid version of XMind costs $79, which is not very expensive, but is not exactly an impulse buy, either. This program does have a nice user interface and a few other features that might be worth it to some.

One of the greatest things about XMind is that it allows for online sharing. This is especially helpful if you collaborate a lot with others. You can share your mind maps online, and when your colleagues (or whoever) go in and edit it, the changes show up on both ends. Another great feature is that there is an iPad version of XMind. So, you can edit your mind maps either on your computer or your iPad. Furthermore, since you do have the online sharing, all your mind maps are always going to be accessible no matter where you are.

The premium option listed above is going to be MindJet. This is very expensive. It costs just under $400. There are subscription options that can be less costly, however. This is a top-of-the-line program. It has the most features out of all the options listed above. Also, the program is designed to help you as you create your mind maps. It is simply much better than most other options. One of its best features is that it contains business collaboration tools which are much better than other programs provide. That is really what makes it worth its premium price to some.

iMindMap is another paid option that is available. One great thing about this program is that it was created by Tony Buzan. He is considered by many to be the creator of the modern day mind map. This program is very similar to XMind in its features and cost. However, it also includes courses on Mind Mapping. Plus, it contains more icons, many of which Tony references in his course. So, this may be the most preferred option if you are a follower of Mr. Buzan. Plus, there are versions of this program available for your iPhone or iPad, and this program provides you with online collaboration tools as well.

MindMeister is a little bit different. It is a completely online tool. In fact, it is a web-based Flash program. So, there is no software to install and it is very inexpensive. It costs about $3 to $15 a month, depending on what features you need and how many people need to have access to your mind mapping program. A disadvantage of this program is that it does require internet access. This program also has IOS and mobile version, but you do need to be able to connect to the Internet in order to access it.

MindMeister will integrate with certain online services, such as Google Drive. So, you can store your maps on Google Drive. A lot of people like options such as MindMeister and Google Drive because they allow you to store your information in 'The Cloud,' where your data is safe from hard drive failures, power surges, and loss. Plus, it is accessible from anywhere this way.

	Price	Advantages	Disadvantages
Freemind	Free	Completely Free Offers most basic features	Interface isn't as nice Can be buggy
XMind	Free Basic Version	More features that Freemind Unlimited Maps	Limited export abilities (free version)
MindJet	$349	Online collaboration Business discount Best User Interface	Expensive
iMindMap	$99 - $249	Created by Tony Buzan iOS/Andriod Versions Online Syncing	Expensive
MindMeister	Free – Limited to three maps	No software to install Good feature set	Requires internet access Limited to 3 maps in free version

Use the chart above to help you make your choice. However, in the short term, please just find and download a copy of FreeMind. This way, those who have purchased this book will have the opportunity to go out and get this software without having to purchase anything extra. That is why the author chose FreeMind and recommends its use to anyone who is trying to get started in mind mapping.

If you find that FreeMind doesn't suit your needs, or if mind mapping becomes an intricate part of your business, then you may want to look into finding programs with online collaboration tools, and so on. For now, attempt to become well-versed in FreeMind in order to get mind mapping down; you will likely find that it contains 90% of what you need, if not all.

Chapter 3: Seven Magical Steps to Mind Mapping

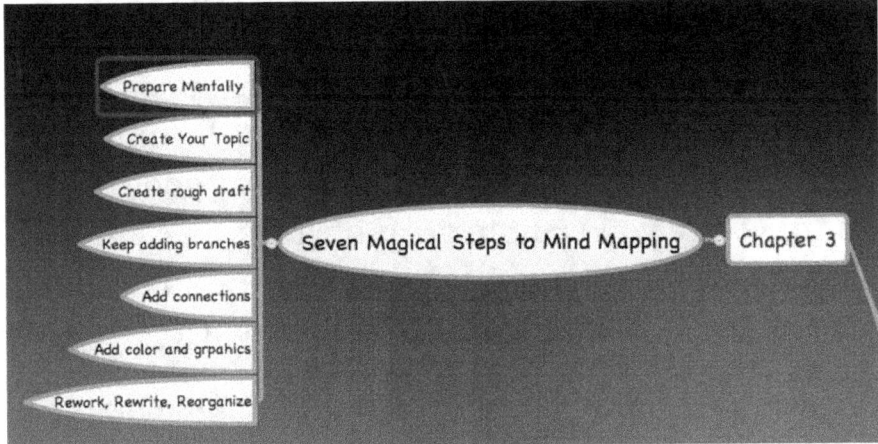

In this chapter, seven magical steps to mind mapping are presented. They will take you all the way from a blank mind map to a fully created one. These magical steps are:

Step 1: Prepare Mentally. You want to begin the process by asking yourself, "What is my goal?" or "What do I want to achieve by creating this mind map?" If this is your first mind map, then you're probably not going to have a very good idea of what you are trying to create. On the other hand, if you have created a mind map before, then you will have a pretty good idea of what your mind map is going to end up looking like. So, why are you doing this? What is the purpose of your mind map, and what do you hope to achieve with it?

You want to have that clear cut goal in mind whenever you create your topic and whenever you branch out into your main topics and your subtopics. The outcome, however, needs to be flexible so that you can use your mind map to explore the topic. Just like a traveler, you may not be completely sure about what the outcome will be, but you should have a pretty good idea of where you want to go and what you want to do before you begin. You don't want to head out aimlessly because you are likely to just get lost.

Keep the following saying in mind: One map, one purpose. You need to create one mind map at a time. Some people have trouble with this idea; without realizing it, they try to cover two topics at once and then things get tangled up because they are too complex. For example, you wouldn't want to create a mind map for 'fruits and vegetables,' you would want to create a mind map for vegetables, and then another one for fruits. You could also have fruits as one node and vegetables as another under one singular topic. In this way, you are able to concentrate on one single topic at a time.

Step 2: Create Your Topic. Once you've decided on a goal and you have chosen your topic, you're going to want to write that topic down in the center of your page. If you are using FreeMind, all you have to do is create a new mind map and type your topic in the center. You can see in the picture above that there is nothing else on the page right now. Everything else is white space.

Your central topic doesn't need to be an entire sentence or an entire paragraph. You should follow the 'three word maximum' rule. You need try to find a way to describe what you're looking for in three words. Sometimes you can't do that, but you want to at least try your best to keep it limited to very, very simple words, and you want to try to use as few words as possible.

Step 3: Create a Rough Draft. Once your
central topic is in place, you want to begin
creating your rough draft. Your rough draft
needs to be black & white, meaning that at this
point you don't need to add images, hyperlinks,
or anything extra. At this point you are not
going to worry about grammar or spelling either.
This way you can really begin cranking it out.
You will learn a little bit more about how this
works in Chapter 4, which covers speed mind
mapping. For now, just understand that doing
this as quickly as possible helps to get your mind
engaged.

You've thought about your topic and so you have
prepared your brain for this task. Now that you
have created your topic, it's time to flesh
everything out. You can worry about taking care
of the red squiggly lines, the errors, and the
images later on. Right now, you just want to get
everything on paper.

Step 4: Keep Adding Branches. Begin to
divide your central topic into pertinent main
topics, keeping your goal in mind as you do so.
Then branch each main topic into subtopics,
taking each as far as you possibly can. The
bigger your mind map becomes, the better this
exercise will work for you. Before you hit a
block, before you get distracted, you want to get

everything you can into that document. You want to flesh this out as much as possible, and you will likely find that once you get your brain going, you won't want to stop. That is good because you don't want to stop until your mind is totally exhausted of all pertinent information.

Step 5: Add Connections. Just let the information flow from your brain, through your hands, and onto the document. Once you let the content flow, and you put everything else out of your mind, you will truly be amazed at what you end up with. When you finally do hit a lull, you want to go through the document and begin adding connections. These connections can be made by adding in dashed lines between your various topics. These dashed lines should be used to demonstrate how the different subjects are connected.

Doing this will get your brain working again and possibly give you a new perspective on the topics that you connect. As you gain these new perspectives, new branches or topics may begin to manifest. If they do, add them in immediately.

Really, if at any time during this process you think of anything new, you should add it in before it escapes your mind. This new topic, or subtopic, may even lead into more branches to add. That is another great thing about computerized mind maps, because if you think of something on the go, it is usually easy to add it into your mind map right then. This is especially true if you generally have access to a computer, laptop, iPad, or the like.

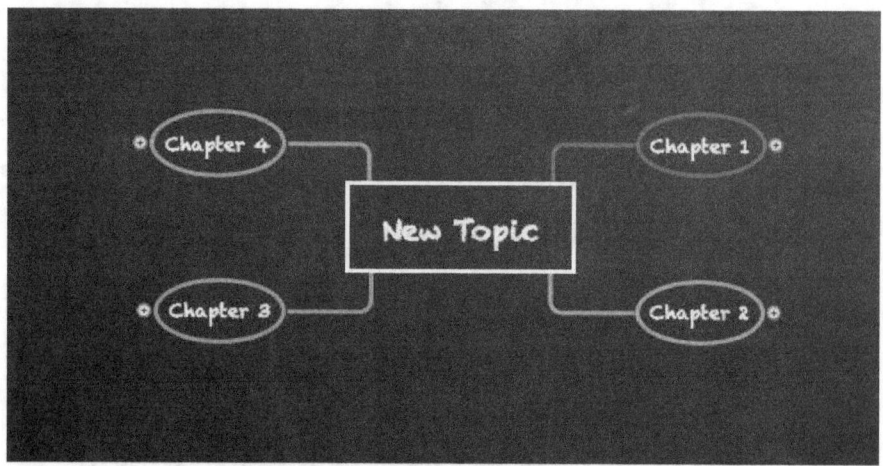

Step 6: Add Color & Graphics. Next, it is recommended that you add color to your mind map to better demonstrate the main topics. So, if you did this to the mind map in the screen shot above, Chapter 1 would be a certain color, Chapter 2 would be a different color, and so on until each chapter was marked with its own color. In your mind each color should represent a connection.

Mind mapping is a very creative process. So, the more color and the more images that you use, the better off you'll be. If there is a topic that you can't think of the word for, just add a graphic to represent it. In fact, some people recommend that you use a graphic in place of a word anytime that you can because it helps you understand, review, and retain the information more quickly.

If you hear someone say the word 'orange', the color or the fruit would usually come to mind in the form of a picture, not the word. That is generally how the human mind works. So, the more images and the more colors that you add to your mind map, the better off you are going to be. It is also going to be easier for you to make associations between the various topics. This is because your brain works through images, symbols, connections, and relationships.

Step 7: Rework, Rewrite, Reorganize.
Since your focus during the mind mapping process is on putting down as much content as you can, revision and editing should be kept to a minimum. Once you feel you're winding down, you can start to prune and rewrite things. Also, at the end, don't be afraid to add more branches and topics. Take advantage of every opportunity you have to add more to your mind map because the more fleshed out it is, the more you are going to be able to learn from it, and the more other people are going to be able to learn from it.

Those are the 'Seven Magical Steps to Mind Mapping'. To break this down for you a little more simply, they are:

1. Prepare Mentally

2. Create Your Topic

3. Create Your Rough Draft

4. Keep Adding Branches

5. Add Connections

6. Add Color & Graphics

7. Rework, Rewrite, Reorganize

Chapter 4: Speed Mind Mapping

In this chapter, you are going to be taking all that you have learned thus far and applying it to a method called 'Speed Mind Mapping'. Speed Mind Mapping involves using those seven magical steps that you learned in the previous chapter to get your brain to come up with the information that you need and organize it as quickly and as effectively as possible.

Speed Mind Mapping was referenced when the seven magical steps were being covered, but now you are actually going to learn how to do this. Before you begin, you will want to review the seven magical steps. When you are speed mind mapping, you are going to focus primarily on the first three or four steps, and the main one to focus on is the third: Create Your Rough Draft. That is really the basis of speed mind mapping. The point is to create your content and get it into your mind map as quickly and as effectively as possible.

The first thing that you are going to do, as previously stated, is take a moment to identify what the actual purpose of the mind map is and prepare yourself mentally to begin. This will help you to know what your central topic should be. In this case, the purpose of the mind map being created is to demonstrate the process of Speed Mind Mapping, so the central topic of the mind map being created is 'Mind Mapping'.

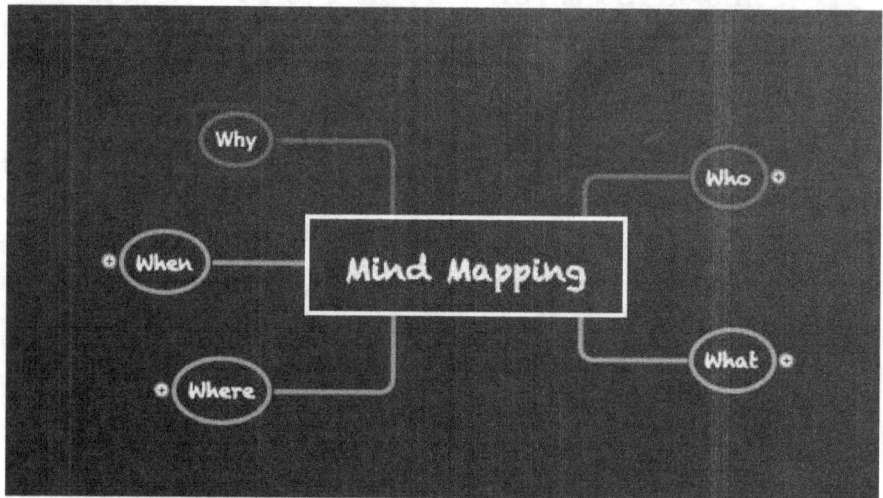

The next step is to begin inputting your main topics. In the example above, you can see that these are:

- Who

- What

- Where

- When

- Why

- How

These make great main topics for most mind maps because they are easy to think up, and they usually cover just about everything. As the mind map was being made, its creator did not worry about spelling or anything of the like. He just began adding to the mind map as quickly as possible as different things popped into his head. In the beginning, you should do the same.

If you are creating a mind map for a topic that you don't know much about, the process is probably not going to go very quickly for you. In most cases, however, the 'name of the game' is speed. You are going to want to put all of this together as quickly and efficiently as possible. As soon as a word comes to your head, write it down. You may need to add more sub-nodes as your thoughts about a particular topic grow. Just go wherever your mind takes you and continue branching things out.

You want to follow your brain as it works. You will really gain great insight into how your brain works by how it lays out all of these things. You want to allow your mind to sort of work on auto-pilot and you really don't want to stop speed mind mapping until you hit a block. At that point, you will want to begin playing with those connections and adding things as necessary.

After that, you can begin adding in some color and some graphics. Don't be afraid to be a little creative. This will probably spark your interest even further, allowing you to add in even more.

Finally, you will want to go back over everything that you have created in order to rework, rewrite, and reorganize it. Even as you are doing this, when new things come to you, continue to go with it and add more content. If you get tired of doing this, or you hit roadblocks, remember that you can always stop and revisit this in a couple of hours. Sometimes, this even allows your mind to open up to even greater ideas.

The mind will do weird things. Sometimes if you go off and take a walk, or start doing other things, your brain will continue breaking apart problems subconsciously. Sometimes you go to bed with a problem and wake up with the solution: hence the phrase, "sleep on it."

Sometimes you may even be working on something completely unrelated, and all of a sudden something sparks new interest in your mind about the problem that you were mind mapping about. For example, you may be working on a car in your garage, and the entire time your mind is subconsciously thinking through your mind map. Then, all of a sudden you are able to see the problem in a different light. You later apply this to your mind map, and things fall right together. The mind is a mysterious thing, and things really can come about in this manner.

It is better to finish your mind map all in one sitting, if you can. You mind works more insightfully and more creatively if it is allowed to work freely, quickly, and without hesitation. Also, if you continue to allow it to move along a path, different things can unfold. However, if you get stuck, sometimes it is best to lay things down and give your mind some time to work through things.

Some people find that when they move things around on a mind map, they can see the relationships between things more clearly and differently. That is another reason why it can really be advantageous to revisit and rework your mind maps.

Chapter 5: Mind Map Templates

There are many, many ways that you can use mind maps. In this chapter, some mind mapping templates are going to be demonstrated. These templates will serve as examples that will hopefully spark your interest and get you thinking about what exactly you can do with these mind maps.

The first template is a basic template. This type of mind map is what was used in all of the examples earlier. This type of mind map starts with a central topic and branches out into main topics and sub topics.

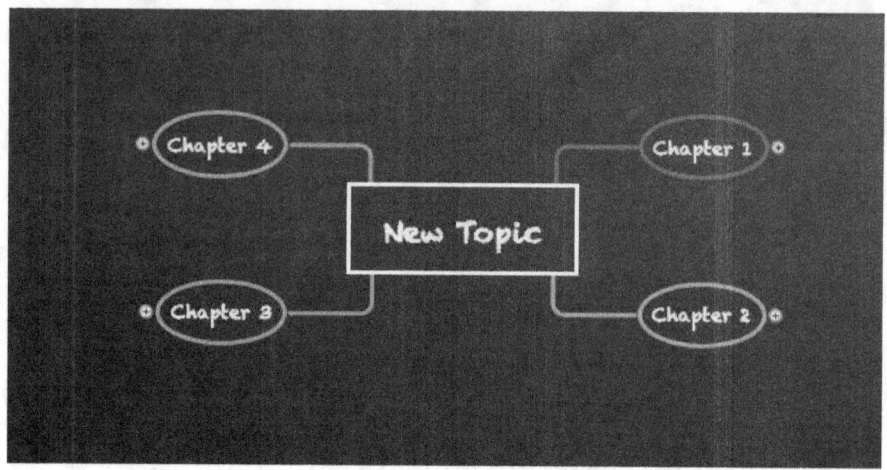

You may notice that each one of these main topics is a different color. As they branch off, each subtopic should remain the color of the main topic from which it spawned. That way, your thoughts stay cohesive both in your mind, and on your mind map. It also makes the mind map look pleasing to the eye.

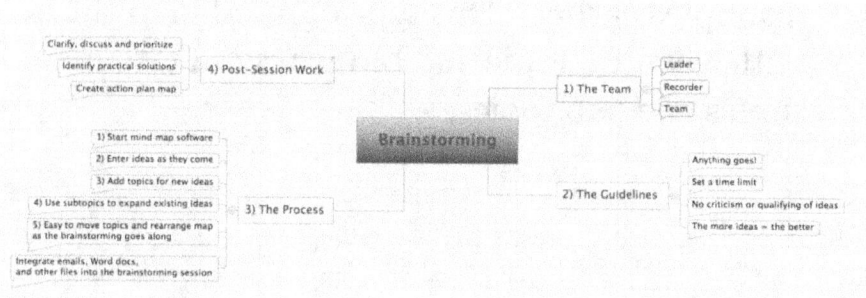

The mind mapping template above is a little bit different than the first. This is a brainstorming template. You'll notice that it carries some of the same elements as your basic template. For example, it begins with a central topic, from which other information branches off. You can use this type of mind map for brainstorming, but it is typically used for project management.

Looking at the picture above, you may notice that your first main topic is 'The Team'. The sub-topics branching off of this is a list of what that team consists of. The second main topic is 'The Guidelines', and branched off from that are the guidelines that the team members are to go by. This mind map also breaks down the process and the post-session work. Hopefully, you can recognize how this mind map is going to help this team to collaborate with each other. The entire process is broken down for them so that everyone understands what their place is and what they should be trying to accomplish step-by-step.

Before presenting a mind map to your team, you may want to start off with something a little simpler than this. The reason is that this may throw some people off or even scare them if they are more used to being fed information through lists or even PowerPoint presentations. So, there may be a little bit of a learning curve at first, but once your team gets the hang of it, they will probably love it as much as you do. In the very beginning you will want to walk them through this mind map, however. The easiest way to teach them is probably to create one together in a team meeting.

In order to present this idea at a team meeting, you can use a computer and a projector. You can hand draw this on a whiteboard or a chalkboard. You will want to outlay this with your team, and walk them through the process. At the same time, instead of taking linear meeting notes, you can have them draw out the mind map on a sheet of paper as well.

Doing this is going to help your team in two different ways. First, it is going to get them involved, which means that they are going to learn more from the actual experience. Secondly, this is going to allow you to combine everyone's ideas all at once. People learn a lot more from a mind map than they do from the more typical linear type of notes.

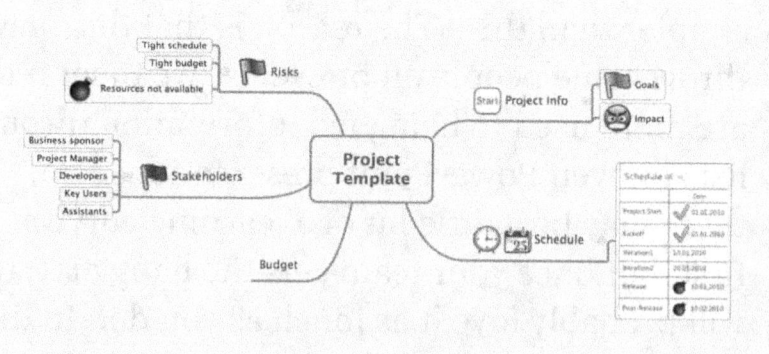

Above is another mind map template. It is a time/project management template. This is a great template to use because it allows you to outlay the entire project as well as schedule everything. You can also put everyone's stake in the job into this mind map.

Say, for example, a client calls up and asks how things are going with a particular project. Well, you can instantly load this up and immediately see all of the green checks, red Xs, and so on. That is one reason why it is recommended that you use icons, so that you can process the information quickly and easily.

You may notice, in the template above, that the 'Release' and 'Post-Release' is marked with bomb icons. The 'Project Start' and 'Kickoff' are also marked, this time with green check marks. This, of course, symbolizes that they are done. If you run into a problem, you can use a bomb icon to symbolize that, or a bomb might be used to represent a deadline or anything else. The red dashed icon in FreeMind is often used to represent importance. There are also number icons in FreeMind which are useful when prioritizing different tasks.

You can use these icons in whichever way you feel best communicates the information. It is recommended that you keep using the same icons to represent the same thing each and every time. This way you are communicating clearly, there is no confusion, and the information can be taken in at a glance. You will also want to add every topic, every subtopic, and every to-do onto this mind map. That will give you a better idea and a better understanding of the entire project as a whole.

If you break the tasks down and add time limitations to each task, you will be able to have a loose estimate of how long the project should take. At the same time, you will have an ongoing status update on the project. Say, for example, you posted a template like this and gave access to all of your employees to be able to change and edit it. You can simply open this up throughout the day to see what has gotten done and what hasn't. They can also add in notes and icons to symbolize different things. For instance, an employee could throw a bomb in if they run into a problem. You will be able to see this too, and you will, therefore, know to call and check on the problem.

So, this could essentially be a huge overlay of massive communication for you, if you wanted it to be. You could manage a ton of employees, for example, without having to talk to anyone and without having to read a thirty-page email update. This simply outlays the project a lot better.

The next template is a studying template. It was made to be used by students, but it can be utilized in a number of different ways. This is designed to put the central topic, for example Critical Literature, in the middle, and then you would outlay all of the major topics and subtopics on top of that. You may notice that in this template, like the basic template, all of the different branches are different colors.

You may also notice that one of the branches on the left has a bubble around it, and that is because it is a critical review outline. So, everything on the right is your research, and the portion on the left is your outline. This could, therefore, not only help you study, but also to write out an essay. It also allows you to more easily see how all of the different topics relate to each other, and you can easily draw out even more connections if needed.

The mind mapping process will probably be a little bit slower when you are first starting out. You probably have years of experience taking linear notes, whether you do this on a computer or on a piece of paper. So, when you first start learning to mind map, it is not a bad idea to take your notes in the linear fashion you are used to and then transfer them onto a mind map. Then as you become more experienced with mind mapping, you can replace your linear style of notes with mind maps.

Transferring your linear notes gives you another opportunity to review the information that you are trying to learn again. This way you can wrap your mind around the various concepts and facts, and you may even be able to make better connections between them as you do so. Also, you may remember things that were discussed in class that you did not get into your notes the first time around. This can be a very effective way to study, as it has been proven that reviewing information shortly after it is first discussed makes it stick in your brain better.

Mind maps are also great to use if you are in a study group. A good way to use them is to have everyone take notes and then create a mind map out of them before they come to the study group session. Then, when everyone gets together, you can take all six of those mind maps and create a new giant mind map out of them. When you put all of those different ideas and perspectives together, you are going to have a much greater understanding of the information at hand. This will also help to ensure that you didn't miss anything. Furthermore, this is going to get everyone involved, and so the learning process is going to be that much stronger.

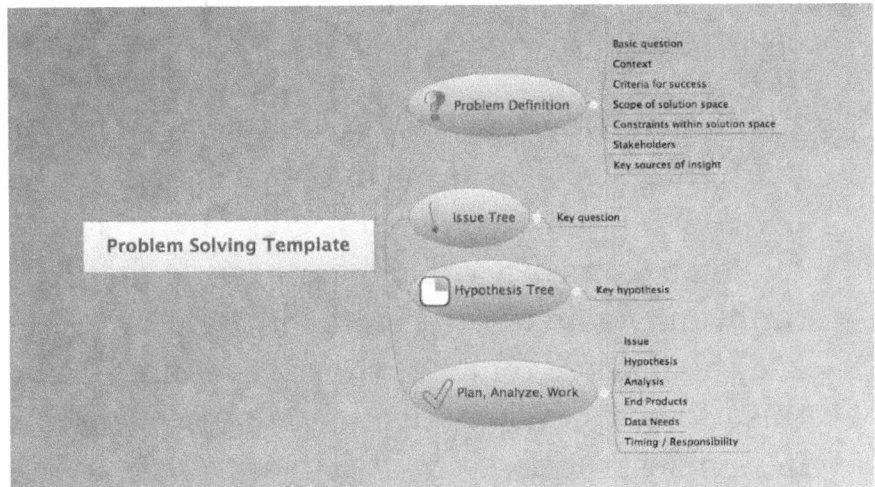

Above is the 'Problem Solving Template'. There are four main topics on this problem solving template. These are labeled as followed:

1. Problem Definition

2. Issue Tree

3. Hypothesis Tree

4. Plan and Analysis and Work

This mind mapping template is very useful when it comes to solving very difficult problems, whether they are scientific problems, math problems, or life problems. This mind map forces you to break down a problem into its parts. When you are using this mind map it is recommended that you use short keywords. If a topic requires more than 3-5 words, then you should consider creating a new line for it. You may also consider breaking up a single topic into various subtopics.

In the issue tree, you want to outline all of the different issues you see with the problem. By breaking up the problem, it is going to be easier for you to come up with a hypothesis to that problem. Again, it is recommended that you keep all of these topics as short as possible, as this will help you to understand the problem in its simplest form.

The hypothesis tree is probably the most important part of this mind map. This is, of course, where you state what the problem is and write out your assumption. You would probably want to break the three-word rule here and clearly state your position. However, everything else being broken down as simply as possible is going to help you to create your hypothesis as well as make a better analysis. You should also jot down the results of your analysis in the simplest way possible.

One great thing about this template is that it allows you to go back and rework things quickly and easily. If your hypothesis ends up being incorrect, for example, you can look over all of this to be sure that there is nothing that you missed. It also would help you to spot other things that may have skewed your results. Also, if you save your mind map before changing it each time, you will have an accurate record of what you did and did not do.

Five useful and productive ways of using a mind map have been outlined herein. Hopefully, this sparked some information and will help you move forward with mind mapping. As you can see, there are no limitations to what you can do with a mind map. Any of these examples are useful, some more so than others in certain situations. In any case, these can all be useful in no matter which type of problem you need solved. Hopefully, these templates will help to make your life much simpler.

Chapter 6: Moving Around Your Mind Map

Now you know the basics of creating a mind map, and you should have something on paper at this point. You may have some of your thoughts and ideas on paper. You may even have some color and some graphics here and there. If so, you have a pretty developed mind map.

In this chapter, you are going to learn about moving around your mind map. The most obvious way to do so is by using the scroll bars. In FreeMind you have scroll bars that move left and right and scroll bars that move up and down. If you have your mind map fully branched out, you may have to navigate through it in this way.

The program also allows you to view it differently by zooming in and out. You can do this by clicking on 'View' and then, of course, 'Zoom In' or 'Zoom Out'. From the 'View' menu, you can also click on 'Rectangular Selection' to draw a selection.

When you look inside the 'View' menu, you may notice that beside the 'Zoom In' and 'Zoom Out' options are the keyboard shortcuts. You can also use your keyboard to navigate around the mind map. You can simply use your arrow keys to do so, just like you would in most other programs. You can also use your space bar to expand and contract the various branches.

There are a few more keyboard shortcuts that you can use in FreeMind if you are not the 'point and click' type. For example, the edit option is F2. So, if you click F2 you are going to be able to edit the text of one of your branches. If you want to replace your current text, you can just start typing, and you can replace what was previously there with what you typed.

The keyboard shortcuts that you use are going to depend on whether you are editing or creating your mind map. For example, you are not going to use the up and down arrows when you are creating because you are going to be using the 'Tab' and the 'Enter' keys (Mac) or the 'Insert' and 'Enter' keys (Windows) to create your mind map a little more efficiently.

Using your mouse is only one way to get information into your mind map. The quickest way to do so is to use your keyboard. So, all of your applications are going to contain different keyboard shortcuts. This is true for any program that you choose to use. The easiest way to figure out what shortcuts to use is by clicking on the 'Help' tab. In FreeMind, when you look under the 'Help' tab, you will see 'Key Documentation PDF'. You can click here to see what keyboard shortcuts are available for this program. MindJet's options are very similar to FreeMind's, by the way.

Another way to figure out what keyboard shortcuts are available is to open up the various menus and look at the different menu options. Most mind mapping programs will list your keyboard shortcuts alongside your menu options. So, once you get a little bit quicker at using the program that you have chosen, you can view your keyboard shortcuts and begin using them.

You can try this now, if you like. Say, for example, that you wanted to add another chapter to the mind map pictured above. All you would have to do is select the chapter that you wanted it to follow and then hit 'Enter' and a new 'Main Topic' branch will appear. If you wanted to create a new subtopic instead, you would hit 'Tab' and a child node will appear for the chapter selected. To add another node onto the same branch, you would hit 'Shift+Tab'. These are the typical shortcuts that you will use when you are creating a mind map.

If you are editing or adding to a mind map, you will be using some of the shortcuts listed above. Most of the time, however, you will be using your arrow keys to navigate around your mind map and the spacebar to expand and contract everything as needed. Again, you can use your mouse and the scroll bars to navigate through your mind map, but using your keyboard shortcuts is significantly faster.

There is not a keyboard shortcut for everything in FreeMind. For example, when choosing an icon, you are going to use the icon panel that is on the left-hand side of the program. To do this, you would click on the icon you wanted and it would automatically insert itself into the selected field.

There are simply not enough keyboard shortcuts to make one available for each icon. However, wouldn't it be nice to be able to have a shortcut for some of your favorite icons? Well you can, in fact, do that. By clicking on the 'FreeMind' menu and then choosing 'Preferences' you can change your keyboard shortcuts. To do this, just click on the 'Keystrokes' button inside of the 'Preferences' window, find the icon that you would like to create a shortcut for, and assign a keyboard shortcut to it by typing what you want into the box next to the icon. If you do this for the icons that you most commonly use, it will make your mind map creation process much faster.

Now you know how to move around FreeMind. The process of moving around other mind mapping programs is very similar, in most cases. You have also learned how to find and learn the available shortcuts, as well as change them if you need to. Try to learn these shortcuts if you can because it really will make the process of creating a mind map a lot faster for you. Remember, the best mind maps come about when you work quickly, creatively, and instinctively.

Chapter 7: Mind Map Tactics 101

In this chapter, you are going to learn some basic mind mapping tactics. These are tactics that you will want to keep in mind whenever you are building a mind map. You will also want to keep these in mind when you are editing your mind maps.

The mind mapping tactic is to learn those keyboard shortcuts and use them whenever possible. Using keyboard shortcuts is going to make the process of mind mapping a lot simpler and you are going to be able to create mind maps far more efficiently. Again, you can find out what the keyboard shortcuts in FreeMind are by clicking on 'Help' and then choosing the 'Key Documentation PDF'. You can also choose 'Help...' and 'FAQ' from the 'Help' since they also contain information about what shortcuts are available.

Another easy way to go about finding out what shortcuts are available is by clicking on the 'FreeMind' menu and then choosing 'Preferences'. Doing so will open up a menu where you can click on the 'Keystrokes' button and look over, and even change, the keystroke options. So, for example, if you wanted there to be a shortcut that will insert one of the icons, you can create one by setting your preferences within this window.

Make sure you learn your keyboard shortcuts because this is going to allow you to speed up the mind mapping process immensely. When mind mapping, speed is your friend. You want to make sure that you get all the information onto your mind map first. Yes, this has been stated before. However, this is one of the most important things to remember when you are mind mapping. You want to keep your brain cranking because this forces the brain to think things up, but in a way that opens your mind up and allows thoughts to come about freely. This is how the most creative and deep thoughts come into play.

Once you hit a lull and the ideas on what to add aren't coming to you as quickly, then you can look at the spelling and begin adding in images, colors, icons, and so forth. As you do so, you will probably become reengaged and will be able to add even more to your mind map. Then all you have to do is go over it once more in order to edit and rework the information.

Don't forget that mind mapping is a very personal process. After all, you are just allowing your thoughts to go onto paper as quickly as they come to you. This allows the purest of your thoughts to be put onto paper without fear of judgment or being reprimanded. These thoughts just go straight from your mind to the paper, without anything else coming into play.

That is why, at times, the process of mind mapping can feel really freeing to people and often relieves stress. Mind mapping quickly allows you to get all of those daily problems and roadblocks out of the way and allows your mind to act freely. While doing so, however, it allows you to focus on one task at a time.

Your brain is amazing. It is capable of defining relationships between all of these different topics. Your brain works best when it is allowed to make connections in this way. That is why mind mapping works so well. However, it is a very personal process that works best when you preclude any forethought. So, if you are going to share your mind maps, you will want to be sure to rework them beforehand to ensure that everyone else can understand.

Since mind mapping is so personal, whatever works best for you is the best way to go about creating a mind map. Just like each painter has his own methods when creating his art, you will develop your own personal mind mapping tactics. You want the information going straight from point A, your brain, to point B, your hand, to point C, the paper or the digital mind map.

Even though the mind mapping process is very personal, it is amazing what occurs when you mind map as a group. All of the dynamics of that group fall into the creation of that mind map, and you will get some insight into how everyone's mind works. This process will review things to you, and to them, that you didn't know before, either about the topic or about each other.

As you create various mind maps, you will want to stay consistent in how you do so. For example, the icons that you use should always mean the same things to you. You should be consistent with the colors every time, as well. That way everything will make perfect sense to you at a glance, and you won't always have to rethink everything.

When you share your mind maps with other people, you will want to be sure to define what all of these symbols mean because, of course, what means one thing to you, may mean something else in someone else's mind. So, if you use a bomb, for example, to represent something that is broken or something that needs to be fixed, then you don't want to use the stop sign to represent the very same thing, at times. The symbolism needs to be clear, concise, and consistent every time, particularly if you are trying to communicate with others.

Again, when you create your mind maps, you want to be consistent with your icons and your colors so that your brain instantly recognizes the meaning of each. This is even more important when you are sharing mind maps with others. They need to be able to get used to those icons and know what each means without having to question. If you are creating mind maps as a group, you want to give people the freedom to express themselves, but you don't want to allow people to change the way that the icons are used. This way there is no confusion when it comes to what these symbols mean.

Chapter 8: Advanced Tactics

In this chapter, you will be provided some advanced tips, tricks, and tactics for making your mind mapping experience better, quicker, and more efficient. One tactic that will help you immensely is to create a 'Master Mind Map'. To create a master mind map, all you do is create a new map and use it as a giant server for the rest of your maps.

The Master Mind Map. Say, for example, you generally do mind maps for work, home, and vacations. Your central topic could then be your name, and then you make work, home, and vacations your main topics. Then, you can simply add branches onto each for all of your individual mind maps. This way you only have to bring up one document to find whatever mind map you're looking for. If you would like, you can also add in more subtopics in order to better organize your mind maps. This way you can have your entire collection of mind maps organized into various categories, in other words.

Doing this will allow you to have everything together, but at the same time, you can do the same things with your master map as you can do with each individual map. For example, you can develop relationships between your mind maps and notarize those on your master map. So, this is one tactic that is very easy to implement, and it will get everything straight for you. This way you don't have to search through the computer to find the mind map you're looking for. You can simply link to them through this master mind map.

To add links to you master mind map, all you have to do is click on 'Insert' and then choose one of the 'Hyperlink' options from this menu. The 'File Chooser' is what you will most likely use. This will allow you to add any files that you like. Once you do this, you will notice that there is an arrow added to your master mind map. Clicking this arrow will open up the file that you have designated. The 'Text Field' hyperlink option will allow you to link into a website. You can also link into various files on your computer by using the 'Add Graphical Link' and 'Add Local Hyperlink' options under that same 'Insert' menu.

Using Tablets & Mobile Devices. The next advanced tactic that you can use is to implement your iPad and mobile devices into your mind mapping activities. In today's mobile world, there are a lot of mind mapping applications available for your use. So, now you can mind map on your iPad, iPhone, Android, etc. These, of course, will allow you to mind map 'on the go' and jot down all of your ideas as they strike you.

Some might say "Well, I can just do that on my laptop." However, until you try it, you really don't realize how convenient this is. Most people keep their phones on them all of the time and so this allows you to jot things down more quickly and while your ideas are fresh on your mind.

Tablets are usually more accessible than a laptop as well. This is great because tablets really give you the best of both worlds, meaning that you get the physical interaction like you would with a piece of paper, but you are putting it into a physical format as well. Furthermore, a lot of these applications will sync back to your desktop, where you can access it later if you need to.

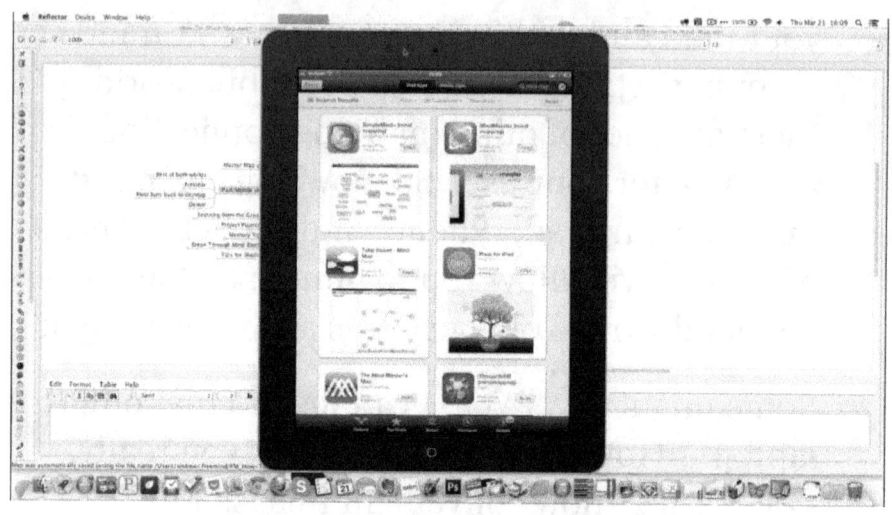

There are a plethora of iPad applications out there, kind of like these. Some of these applications are shown in the picture above. Some of the applications that are available are free, but they may have a limitation on them. The one most recommended by this book's author is iThoughtsHD. It is the most popular among people who use mind mapping software, and it's free.

If you use a certain program on your computer, you may want to use an app that compliments that. For example, if you use MindJet, then there is an app specifically made for this program. This app is demonstrated in the picture below. You can create a new map by clicking and dragging to one side or the other.

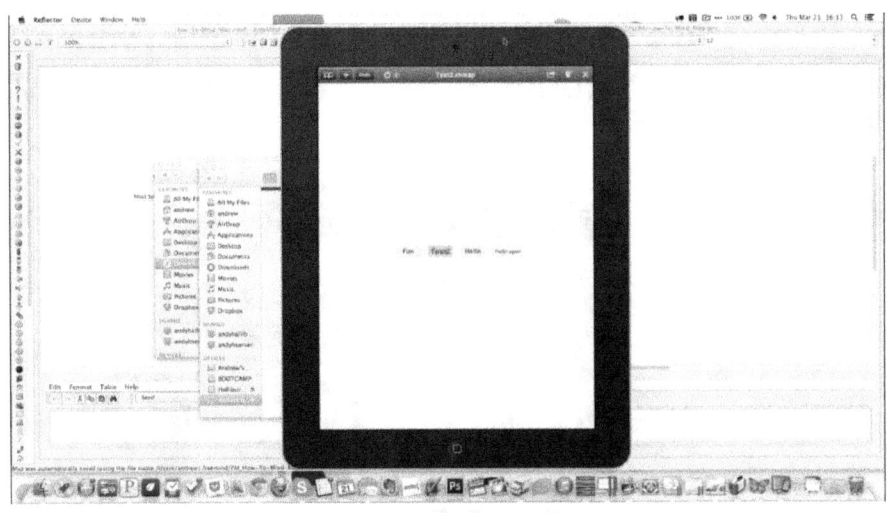

As you save your mind map, it is synced automatically in 'the cloud'. So, when you get back to your desktop computer, all of the mind maps that you have created are accessible. This gives you the ability to work on your mind maps in a meeting or any other time you are away from your desk.

These applications often give you the same options as your typical mind mapping programs do. For example, you can do things like change the color of various topics. In this particular program, when you change the color of one topic, the entire branch changes color, as well. This entire process is not unlike the process you follow when you are at your desktop. However, in this case, you are actually touching the display; so you are able to manipulate this mind map in ways that you can't with your computer.

This is why it was said that a tablet gives you the best of both worlds.

A tablet gives you the ability to test and play with your mind maps on a more personal level. Yet, at the same time, you still have all of the computerized options available to you. Creating a mind map on a tablet, therefore, may actually be the most optimal way to do so for some.

In any case, once you become very proficient in mind mapping, it is recommended that you try out one of these mind mapping applications for your mobile device, tablet, or both. Again, this will give you the ability to continue mind mapping, even when you are away from your computer.

It is also recommended that you use mobile devices for mind mapping because you can use them in different places. For example, you can take these devices outside and work on your mind maps as you relax on the porch. Mind mapping in this type of relaxed state and calm environment will allow you to think more clearly and more proficiently.

On the other hand, you can take it to a job site and possibly get a better outlook on a project. For example, if you were going to overlook the progress of a construction site, you can use your iPhone mind mapping app to take notes while you're there. That is one thing that makes these applications so nice. They give you the ability to add to your mind maps whenever you are not at home.

Learning from the Greats. It is simply human nature to try to learn from people who are very smart and/or extremely efficient. This is how people leverage the knowledge of others so that they can become better, smarter, and quicker. One of the things that you can do is look for 'Mind Maps that Speak,' so that you can model after them. There are certain elements that people have discovered work best in mind mapping. Based on these ideas, the perfect mind maps will:

- Fit your end goal

- Include colors and images that add to its purpose

- Be clean and well designed

- Make sense

- Flow well

- Be portable

- Be compact

- Be easily understood by outsiders

- Provide outside links

- Provide a return on ideas

First of all, you want to look for a map that fits your end goal. This is especially true when you are searching for templates. Whether you have created a map yourself on a piece of paper or from a template, make sure that your map fits the end goal that you envisioned when you followed those seven magical steps. If it doesn't, either rework it or find another template.

Templates are great because often times they are available for free online. So, you can find a whole lot of different templates at no cost that you can use in a variety of different ways. For instance, you can find one easily that is made specifically for problem solving. A lot of the templates that were demonstrated in Chapter 5 will get you started with most types of projects; however, there are a lot more templates out there that may suit your particular needs better. A good mind map should completely fill the purpose that it was designed for.

In addition, you want your mind map to include colors and images that add to its purpose or end goal. You want these images to mean something to you and to your intended audience. If you have an audience that will view your work often, then you will want to remain consistent with these colors and images. If you have a system of your own, it is best for you to stick with that system as well. However, there are certain scenarios where you can look to other mind maps for inspiration on how they use their colors and images. This may help you to create better mind maps for certain situations in the future.

There is no sense in using images that are not in line with your goals. Don't just use images for images sake. You should only use images that help you to achieve whatever you are trying to accomplish or communicate with your mind map. The point of using images in a mind map is not to make them look fancy. The purpose is to make your mind map help you, and your audience, take in information more quickly and sometimes at a deeper level than before.

Another thing to keep in mind is that a clean and well designed mind map is going to go a lot further than a busy and unorganized mind map. For example, even though the basic mind map shown in Chapter 5 was more creative and included more images than most, every color or picture had a purpose and it was not cluttered. Mind maps have to make sense and they have to flow well. Those two things go hand in hand.

Ultimately, you want someone who is a newbie at mind mapping to be able to pick up your mind map and understand what it means without anything having to be explained. If someone has never seen a mind map at all before, you may have to explain how one works, but you shouldn't have to explain the content. For the most part, it should be self-explanatory by design.

You also want your mind maps to be portable and compact. You may have noticed in the previous examples that each line of the FreeMind mind map shown has a circle at the end. Clicking on these circles will allow these lines to collapse or expand. This, of course, allows the mind map to become more compact. It is also important in most cases for your mind map to be portable, especially when you want it to be shared.

Obviously, you will want your mind map to be easily understood by outsiders. This goes back to the point that it should be easily understood by design. It also reinforces the point that your mind map should be clean, neat, and uncluttered. Again, be sure to only use images that contribute to its purpose.

One of the greatest advantages of using computerized mind maps is that you can insert outside links. For example, if you wanted to further a point by inserting a link to a YouTube video, you absolutely could. You can also add in documents and images this way.

Say that you are designing a website for someone, for instance. You could add links to good websites that work as examples of what you want to do. Showing this to your client may help the process to move along easier. It doesn't always make sense to add an image to the mind map. Again, you want things to stay compact, clean, and neat. Sometimes outside links will work much better.

A great mind map will always provide an ROI. In this case, ROI doesn't mean return on investment, it means return on ideas. A good mind map should keep your ideas flowing, in other words. It should keep your brain engaged and keep your brain thinking of new angles and new ways of adding new ideas, new topics, new subtopics, etc.

Project Planning. Using mind maps for project planning is an advanced tactic. It's an advanced idea, but once you use it, once you embrace it, you'll love it because it makes your project planning, the execution, and the completion of the project a lot simpler. You can throw in factors such as:

- Scope

- Time

- Cost

- Quality

- Risks

- Communication

- Resources

Using a mind map for this tactic takes a little bit of getting used to, but once you learn how to do this you will see how useful it is. You will like it a lot because it gives you a 'thirty-foot view', but at the same time it allows you to get into the smaller details of a project. It also allows you to keep up with the project because you and your team members can check everything off as you go.

Memory Tips. Most people know that for something to be committed to memory, you must run through it at least three times. The mind map allows you to quickly review information again and again. Your mind also works by making connections, and mind maps work in this way as well. The mind map helps you to build relationships between things.

If you are using mind maps to study, for example, you can listen to your instructor, write linear notes, and then transfer them to the mind maps. There you go; you have reviewed the information three times. However, you can even take things a step further by reviewing your mind map a time or two before your exam, or you can take it to your study group and expand upon it with them. Furthermore, the fact that the information is put into the simplest form possible helps you to retain the information even more. The fact that the mind map is going to show the relationship between things is going to help you take in and understand the information as well.

Revisit your mind map daily and you will find that the information in the mind map just sticks into your brain. Doing so will also give you a fresh perspective on the things included in your mind map. It will also help you to reconsider things as they change and it will remind you of things that you may have forgotten.

Break Through Mind Blocks. Mind maps can help you to break through mind blocks as well. This is a problem that many of us have to face day to day, and a problem which prevents us from accomplishing as much as we could. There are four different tactics that you can use to break through those mind blocks. They are:

1. Leave Topics Blank – Create blank topics as you mind map. For example, if you are creating a mind map and you cannot think of the name of a main topic that you want to use, then leave a blank there and just add subtopics to it. Sometimes, as you are working the subtopic out, the word will just come to you all of the sudden. If you can't think of it by the end of the mind mapping session, you can look it up later or even create new topics out of your subtopics.

Also, when you leave an empty space on a mind map, your brain is compelled to fill it. So, your brain is going to be working out ways to fill that space, whether you realize it or not. When you don't know something, what do you do? You keep going with what you do know. For example, if you are writing a paper and you don't know how to write the introduction, you write the rest of the paper and come back to the introduction later. That is how you work around your mental blocks.

2. Ask Questions – If you don't know something, write a question on the mind map. Then you can seek the information out later by searching in Google, looking in your text book, and so on. You can also leave a question to be answered when you revisit your mind map tomorrow. Your brain will naturally try to work out the answer while you are away.

3. Add Images - Another way to break through those mind blocks is to add images. For example, if a word is escaping you, you can just use an image to take its place. Go to Google, search for a related word, scroll through the results, and choose the image that best describes what you are trying to think of. Sometimes, when you see an image of something, the name of it comes to mind immediately.

Our brain often works in images. Adding images onto a mind map, therefore, helps the brain to make the associations it needs to make. You don't want to make your mind map too colored, and you don't want to just throw a lot of pointless images onto your mind map, but don't be afraid to add in images that help to bring your messages across, because images help the brain to process information faster.

4. Walk Away - At times, a great way to break through your mind blocks is to simply walk away. If there is something that you can't think of right away, there is nothing wrong with giving it a few hours. Go for a walk, play a game, or whatever, but give it some time. Often your mind will work through problems on its own. Later, when you return to the task at hand, suddenly it all makes sense.

If you return to it, and you can't think of the answer right away, put it off until tomorrow. The answer might suddenly hit you in the shower tomorrow, or you might be sitting with friends and someone says something that brings about the answer in your own mind. The reason why you would even notice this is because your brain is subliminally trying to work it all out. Whatever happens, when you discover your answer, return to your mind map as soon as you can. If you can't do that right away, jot down the answer on a piece of paper so that you don't lose it.

Tips for Sharing. You are probably going to share a lot the mind maps that you will make with others. There are things that you can do that will help you to better communicate what you are trying to say through the mind map. So, here are some tips.

1. Prepare your audience - The first thing that you will want to do is prepare your audience. If you are sending a mind map to someone who has never seen one before, this task can be very daunting. You have to remember that you have a basic foundation of what a mind map is, but a lot of other people don't. So, you will have to think back to when you didn't know anything about mind mapping.

2. Explain - You will first have to explain what a mind map is and what your mind map is meant to be used for, especially if you are planning on sharing it with co-workers or employees of yours. You might have to explain how everything flows. For example, you might have to tell your co-workers to begin by moving around the central topic clockwise and go out from there.

3. Combined Method - You can also use a combined method to explain your mind map. For example, you can take your linear notes and combine them with your mind method so that

the person you are explaining to will have some insight into what you have done. This way you can show how the notes and your mind map relate to each other. This will give your audience a basis of understanding that they are more oriented to and better engage them as well.

4. Learn how they learn. A lot of people are resistant to change, so when you try to introduce them to something as radical as a mind map they will turn away. You have to understand that people have a tendency to try and avoid things that they don't comprehend immediately, and while a lot of people love mind maps, not everyone is going to be open to it. You want to be sure that you are not forcing someone to learn in a way that they don't learn best. If you do this, they are not going to learn very well that way and it is going to be a painful experience for everyone involved.

If someone is resistant, then adhere to their needs. Use the combined method, or find a way to present the information in a way that they can better understand it. Try to figure out how they learn best and help them out.

5. Joint Creation – Sometimes the best way to introduce the use of mind maps to your team is to sit them down in a room and have everyone

create one together. Once they have been involved with this process, they will have a much better idea of how mind maps work. You can simply begin to do this by drawing a circle on the board with a topic inside, or you can use a computer and projector and build a mind map with them using FreeMind.

Chances are your team is going to enjoy a meeting such as this because they will be allowed to become involved, instead of just having to hear you or someone else talk. This will also allow them to see how you get from one topic to the other as you build the mind map and understand how all the information is related. Once they have experienced this, then you can explain how these mind maps can be utilized for better efficiency.

6. Limit Exposure – When you are making your presentation, you want to limit exposure. In other words, if you open up your mind map and it is expanded all of the way out, you are likely going to overwhelm people. Even a small mind map can blow people's minds if they have never been exposed to them before.

Start with just the central topic and slowly expand out from there as you explain things. That is going to allow people who are not used to learning this way or taking in information in this way get adjusted. In other words, feed the information to them slowly; don't give it to them all at once.

Chapter 9: Conclusion

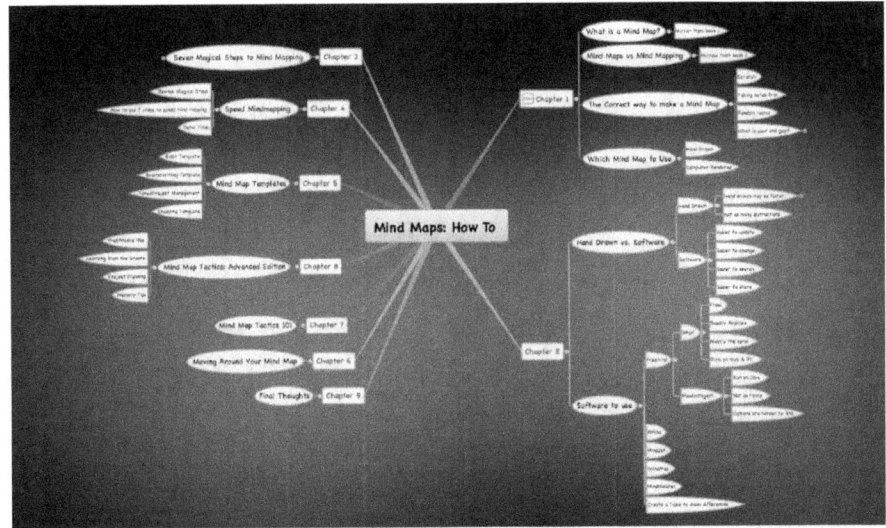

Finally, you have reached the last chapter of this book. In order to bring everything together, let's review the lessons learned.

In Chapter 1, you learned what a mind map is and what it looks like. You probably already knew all of this in the first place, but to recap, a mind map generally consists of:

- A central topic

- A number of main topics

- A series of subtopics

The relationships between these topics and subtopics are usually shown with arrows and/or singular lines. The main topics usually surround the central topic in a circular formation, but not always. The subtopics usually branch out from there, and you can include as many subtopics as needed when mind mapping.

Many people do not realize that there is a difference between mind maps and mind mapping. The best way to think of mind mapping is the verb as opposed to the noun, mind map. In other words, 'mind mapping' is the process of creating a mind map, and a 'mind map' is the final product which derives from the mind mapping process. Finally, you learned that it was important to define what you wanted to achieve by creating a mind map before you begin to create it.

Chapter 2 was basically a breakdown of the different types of mind maps you could use. You also learned about the advantages and disadvantages of hand-drawn versus computerized mind maps. It was established that hand-drawn maps were usually faster, but computerized maps were often easier and more useful. Afterwards, you were informed of some software options that are currently available. It was recommended that you use FreeMind, at least until you get the hang of things. It is a free program and it has most of the same options that many of the premium options have.

The 'Seven Magical Steps' were introduced in Chapter 3. These steps not only walk you through the process of mind mapping, but ensure that you do so in an informed manner. The first and most important step was to prepare mentally beforehand and to have a goal in mind before ever starting. To reiterate, the seven magical steps are:

- Prepare mentally

- Create your topic

- Create rough draft

- Keep adding branches

- Add connections

- Add color and graphics

- Rework, Rewrite, Reorganize

Remember that when you create your rough draft, you want to add the information as quickly as possible and not worry about spelling and so on. You continue adding in this information until you hit a lull and then you can think about looking over everything, fixing things, adding color, adding images, and so on. Finally, you want to rework, rewrite, and reorganize the information as needed. This part of the process may cause you to add a lot more information into the mind map, and so the cycle continues.

Sometimes the process of mind mapping may take a while. Luckily, in Chapter 4 you learned about speed mind mapping. Another thing that will speed things up is using a template, which you learned about in Chapter 5. You also learned how these different templates work. Some of the templates demonstrated were:

- Basic template

- Brainstorming template

- Time/Project Management template

- Studying Template

- Problem Solving Template

In Chapter 6, you learned about moving around your mind maps in FreeMind and in other programs. Hopefully, you understand that in the long-run it is better to learn your keyboard shortcuts. Learning to use them is going to help you to create mind maps more quickly and efficiently. Again, the faster you can create your mind map, the freer, more creative, and less distracted your mind is going to be during this process.

Some basic mind mapping tactics were introduced to you in Chapter 7. In this chapter, the importance of speed and free thought were reiterated, as was the importance of using your keyboard shortcuts.

Finally, you learned about the importance of being consistent. This is particularly true if you plan to share your mind maps with others. However, you should be able to glance at your mind map and immediately know what your symbols mean, so it is important to stay consistent with your own mind maps as well.

Some advanced tactics were shared with you in Chapter 8. One of the best tactics herein is to create a Master Mind Map in order to keep your other mind maps organized and accessible. You also learned how useful tablets and mobile devices could be when it comes to mind mapping. Tablets, in particular, work extremely well as a tool for mind mapping.

In Chapter 8, you learned some established tactics for creating a great mind map. The importance of having a mind map which fits your end goal was covered here, as well as the importance of only using images and colors that help to achieve that goal. You do, however, want to have enough color and images placed within your mind map to keep the mind engaged. A plethora of tactics of how to use and better create mind maps were also included within this chapter.

Hopefully, by reading these chapters, you have learned a lot about the mind maps and the mind mapping process. You should start mind mapping right away, if you have not done so already. Again, you will want to start mind mapping on paper first if you are a beginner, but you will soon be able to move on to mind mapping on your computer, mobile devices, tablets, and so on. You may also be able to convince your boss, employees, team, and other coworkers of how useful the process can be.

At this point, you should go and look at the different software to see which best suits your needs. It is recommended that you try a free version first, at least until you get used to the mind mapping process and get an idea of how often you will actually use it. Also, if you begin with a free option, it will probably be a lot less frustrating starting out. In other words, you might get a little mad if you purchase the $300 version and you don't like it or find that it isn't that much different than the cheaper versions are. Whatever you do, you should get in there, get your hands dirty, and start creating!